My Honest Poem

Jess Fiebig

My Honest Poem

Jess Fiebig

AUCKLAND
UNIVERSITY
PRESS

First published 2020
Auckland University Press
University of Auckland
Private Bag 92019
Auckland 1142
New Zealand
www.press.auckland.ac.nz

ISBN 978 1 86940 924 1

A catalogue record for this book is available from the
National Library of New Zealand

This book was printed on FSC® certified paper

Cover design by Scott Crickett
Book design by Carolyn Lewis

Printed in Singapore by Markono Print Media Pte Ltd

for Kelly Pope
since we were six

Contents

Acknowledgements

Thanks to the editors of the following journals, where many of these poems were published, sometimes in different versions: *Landfall, takahē, Turbine | Kapohau, Poetry New Zealand Year Book, New Zealand Poetry Society, Aotearotica* and *Catalyst*. Thank you also to the judges who commended 'Palmistry' in the 2017 NZPS International Poetry Competition and 'Genetic Conjugation' in the 2018 NZPS International Poetry Competition. I am grateful to Anne Michaels who awarded a collection of these poems Highly Commended in the 2019 Sarah Broom Poetry Prize, and to Fiona Farrell for selecting 'Panic' for inclusion in *Ōrongohau | Best New Zealand Poems 2018*. Special thanks to Gail Ingram whose wisdom, care and direction helped me collate this manuscript. And to the wonderful team at Auckland University Press, especially Sam Elworthy, for making this dream of mine happen.

I would also like to thank my mum, whose support of me telling this story shows real grace.

I have no sense of direction

Maternal Distance

My mother left me at the pier once,
for five hours on a Sunday.
I watched Chinese men gut their fish
in the golden afternoon light,
traced their shadows with the toes
of my shoes, and wondered
        when I would see her again.

I remember her friend colouring
her red hair in our kitchen,
the smell of ammonia
rising from her scalp,
the wet blue slicks of their teeth
from two casks of Velluto Rosso,
the way the silver foils shivered
in her hair as she threw her head back to laugh.

She didn't do that much,
but every now and then spontaneity
tore through her.
Once I found her sitting alone
        at the kitchen table
        blowing bubbles
        in milk through a straw,
giggling as the white froth
spilled over the glass.

She disappeared at Sparks in the Park
one year. I found her passed out
in the back of our old Corolla,
vomit, a collar on her navy woollen jersey
        and no way for us
           to get home.

Life adorned her body:
stretchmarks creeping silver vines
around her abdomen,
freckles on her back
from too much time stoned
        in the sun, I used to trace them
            with my hands.

Bruises bloomed like blue hydrangeas
on her moon-white legs,
a delicate ribbon of broken blood
vessels rose around her neck.

She was quiet, watched half-heartedly,
        from a distance,
            as I grew.

Mum, I am no longer nine years old,
gently brushing your amber hair out
of those great dark eyes, asking if you might
        get dressed,
            go in to work,
                have something to eat?

Eventually,
I stopped imagining
your soft hands resting
on my shoulders, the warm breath
of your whisper.

Years, you would not look me in the eye,
but I could feel
        your stunted love,
            your gaping sadness,
        filling up all the spaces
            between
                us.

Milk Teeth

At eleven I had been walking home for years,
slipping off my shoes in the kitchen,
stuffing wine biscuits into the pockets of my
blue gingham school dress,
                           wandering our flat, looking for
something to do.

The television didn't work
           and often I would find myself
in my mother's closet
           admiring her dresses,
paying special attention to a rust-coloured slip
that shimmered like orange water
                           falling from its hanger.

On her dresser was an empty bottle of perfume,
baby blue with a single red stripe around the stem.
I'd sniff the cap,
           smoky plum and spices,
close my eyes so I might draw my arms around
           her soft neck.

I could sit at the foot of that unmade bed for hours,
turning the bottle gently in my hand,
sunlight making
           its way across the room.

Only once I went through her drawers –
finding treasures I could not explain:
a fake Rolex, an old teaspoon,
and a tiny porcelain box
           filled with milk teeth.

Genetic Conjugation

My grandfather is forever
       explaining etymology
       to busy children,
his favourite, the Latin root
for ambulance,
ambulare, meaning to walk.

He ambles with difficulty,
          tells me he is leaden,
calls me 'girl',
his hugs, rough, awkward
and as he clutches me tightly
I notice that, at 86,
his chest is still firm
      against my cheek,
his woollen sweater coarse and scratchy
over his unsteady heart.

The sugary
     soap smell of daphnes
brings me to his garden
       when I was only small,
plucking clusters of tiny white flowers.
       The scent clinging to my fingertips
pulls me back to
     early mornings eating porridge,
        digging in loamy soil,
        the prickle of kiwifruit skin
and the translucent
     ochre wings of the dead
        monarch butterfly
he kept for me.

Fawns and Foals

Lying on the floor
        legs splayed
you are all long limbs and round, doe eyes,
your shiny hair
        a dark puddle on the carpet

the cadence of your voice has changed
lower, slower,
you tell me about your boyfriend
a surfer, not very smart, but pretty

I think of fawns and foals
first cigarettes, skipped dinners
music reverberating
        through newly emerging hip bones
I recall sixteen tasted
        of orange tic tacs and hunger
fragranced with nail polish, unmixed white spirits
        and vanilla body lotion

your neck is muddy
from clumsily applied concealer

and I think of the photo I saw online
your crop-top, messy topknot,
mixer in hand,
tongue out, peace sign,
a shine in your downcast eyes
that I have seen before,
crumpled sheets on the mattress
        in the background

sixteen is sugar dissolving to salt
on your tongue

            an aftertaste
            that keeps
            repeating,
like breath growing thick and sour
                    in the night.

Dislocation

at six, my mother's boyfriend
forced his fat hairy hand
inside my heart-shaped face
for eating too many Fruit Bursts

we bought a tube of them at BP
wrapped individually in pastel wax papers
which littered the backseat
like sweet-smelling confetti

his hand tasted
of salt
a metallic tang of rust
the hot edge of petrol
from the pump still lingering
on his fingers

with a crack
my lower jaw bone
released from my skull
and he taught me
how to make myself
                 still inside
with another crack
to force it back I learnt
that what this man hated more than
the taffy in my teeth
was women
especially fat ones

my jaw
clicks when I chew
aches when it rains
it is the annex

my social anxieties
hide in
clenched in sleep
until teeth squeak

Spring

Botanical gardens,
tying cherry knots and
admiring pink foxgloves,
the lawn we sit on
imprints criss-crosses,
a map of grass blades
along the backs of my thighs.

His cigarette cherry,
an incandescent maraschino
suspended in twilight,

his picked nails and cuticles
childlike,
but the hands they belong to
are calloused dinner plates
that pull me in,
his grin,
a lesson in something
long forgotten:
warmth.

Picking Cherries

We pick fat, black cherries
that stain our fingertips

jet beads threaded through branches
                          come so easily
                          undone

underneath the adorned canopy
your face;
          dappled,
green light filters through the foliage to
                                trace your features
                     so softly

you place a cherry
                between my open lips
kiss
   the dark sweetness
fermenting inside me –
your mouth is
ripe,
tender fruit.

This is Poetry

I pause our kiss to write a note
about the honeyed whisky
of your tongue
and scrawl up my arm
an explanation as to why
the pine cone
in the table centrepiece
makes me uncomfortable.

I'm up at three
sweeping my mind
for ways to describe the
painfulness of banality,
and the beauty of it too –
certain light, stuck in traffic,
sunshine in the kitchen
when I'm already late for work,
the splash of milk in that fourth cup of tea,
how I chipped your front tooth,
held your thick fingers
and your gaze,
your hyacinth eyes.

This is poetry,
to feel emotions like hot iron
pressing on my skin,
burning to describe the most
complex parts of myself
as simply as I can,
that someone might understand
how scared I am to be alive,
how happy I am to be alive,
how confused I am
when words fly out

of my head like dried butterflies
but how good it feels
to tack their inky bodies on paper
to pin and preserve
the most fragile
parts of myself
and display them
so people I'll never know
can say that my thoughts
were more beautiful
when they flit
through the air.

Hagley Park in Summer

A cicadic chorus,
        trees full of insect gospels,

I feel the greenness
        steady my erraticism,

a rush of calm,
        the lush, softness of it all

the gentleness of unfurling yearnings,
        fronds unwrapping themselves
inside the cage of my ribs.

For Kelly

She wears a crown
of daisies and gypsophila,
hands clasping and unclasping
in nervous excitement,
her shoulders capped with pearls
carefully sewn through dainty lace,
that tiny waist
wrapped in silk-faced satin.

At the end of the aisle,
navy fabric falls down my legs,
and in my sweating hands
yolk-yellow fennel flowers
I see her face,
framed in joy and newly
cropped sand-blonde hair.

I've loved her since we were six,
comparing sandwiches
(hers, a peculiar choice of cream cheese
mine, a more sensible ham).
Her words held such power,
and now
they are vows that will bind her
to a man
who holds her hands
like they are treasure.

Her freckled cheeks
and strawberry mouth
stretch so wide,
like she can't believe,
this is her life.

I get lost in lovers

Dawning

We began on a brisk Sunday morning in May,
standing on uneven gravel
in the middle of a busy carpark

not diluted with wine,
or under the brooding dark
of any Saturday night,
we were caffeinated
in crisp sunlight

your hand,
my cheek

your milky kiss
a tender mouthful
I wanted to
last for
years.

Textures of You

in French Pass
we hunted for crabs
overturning sandstone,
squealing like children

as we made our way
to the next cove,
your rough hands guided me over rocks
their coarseness
gripping my hot shoulders, my back,
cupping my face
in callouses

we swam naked in the green water
your white body firm
against my softness
your mouth was sweet and wet
from riesling,
your stubble a sandy rub
across the delicate skin of
my breasts and neck

afterwards,
edged in salt
we quietly pulled
green-shelled mussels
from the rocks

no sound
but the drag of water on shore
waves pulling the coast
back into itself
again and
again

Divination

It started when the grapefruit tree,
usually laden with orange globes,
grew only four

the house began to smell different
windows unopened,
my grandmother's soft, thin skin
no longer powdered and sweet

when a starling flew inside, its spiny wings
panicked and scratching against the window
she gazed past it,
her hazel eyes following clouds

nestled in eggshells and used tissues,
I found the deep red stones
she wore around her neck
the day my grandfather died,
when I fished them out and asked her
she could not recall my name
but told me that in July 1963
a wasp stung her left thigh
and her life has never been the same

I could hear her dreams through the walls,
of moons and black butterflies,
of newborn babes with long fingers
and worn-out shoes piled high on tabletops.

Tremble

at night a tectonic power
pushed and spread
between us

a tidal tow and shift
that made dogs howl and
earth tremble

but mornings
        were my favourite
dreaming in the wreckage of bedsheets
the sun announcing the day
the warmth of it lying before us

the hand that held my throat
soft in my hair

best of all
the slow waking;

your kisses
so gentle
on my
eyelids.

Shinjuku

I woke sometime between 4 and 5,
that special, still-dark morning time
that lonely lunar mourning time

neon city bursting with
the smell of people, stagnant water, hot oil,
illuminated in its own chaotic charm,

the air head-spin heavy, warm
wrapping around my body like damp, hot wool,
dust and foreign words
clung to the dew of my skin

I could hear the music of our new life
over the electric hum of the city
fighting through fog in my head

Tokyo, suspended in perpetual motion,
never still, far from what I had known –

pale girl, bone-white hair, skin,
soft breasts to stare at –
I was disconnected from the
commute, the standoffish manners,
flashing signs and ten-storey shopping centres
that neighbour temples,
full of peace and incense
where people slow to pour
cool water over their wrists

I am *gaijin*, I am a moth
tapping on the kitchen window
powdery wings making
gentle metallic smudges on the glass

I watch us dancing in the kitchen,
our linoleum ballroom

at the *way of tea*,
businessmen with rumpled suits and smiles
tell me how to cup the bowl
of dark green matcha with both hands,
drink deep

we played out our own tea ceremonies
legs splayed in patches of sunlight,
holding steaming mugs of English Breakfast
Sundays steeped in ritual

I didn't know these moments were perfect;
nothing mattered
but the hot porcelain in my hands.

Saturdays at Bailey's Irish Bar

Saturdays were spent with my stepdad
while mum stayed in bed.
Sometimes, we would listen for hours to
the crack of acorns dropping from tall oaks in the park
as we told stories about
                the cumulus rolling in above us,
sometimes there was backyard cricket
                    or baking strawberry tarts,
but mostly, Saturdays were for pubs
                      with red paisley carpet
where my stepdad would drink Guinness (after Guinness),
each dark stout arriving with a
              heart traced across its head
that I would try to sip,
          the dark, bitter bubbles
so different to the saccharine stickiness in my own glass.

We would sit at the bar,
every now and then a bag of chips appearing,
                a salty appeasement.
Often, we played pool
and though I was too short for the table,
             and scared I might scrape the green felt,
I liked the cue in my hand,
cool and smooth, covered in chalky blue fingerprints
like lipstick smudged on a cheek.

Those afternoons ended with the jukebox,
one of two songs.
Bob Seger meant we would leave in time to catch the bus
then watch onions grow translucent in a pan,
boil spaghetti, grate cheese together –
Seger crooning meant
             laughter, a full tummy, home before six.

The other song was 'Hymn to Her',
Chrissie Hynde's love song to her mother,
which meant we weren't done here,
          that there would be other bars
and waiting outside strange houses –
Hynde meant wandering back from the city
                    under street lights and silence,
the whole eight kilometres my stepdad's fingers linked in
mine,
his middle finger stroking the inside of my palm.

When the red bricks of home would finally come into view,
I could feel Chrissie's words rise inside me,
saw her mother's room, like mine,
                    wallpapered with dreams.

As We Stand Back on Sumner Beach

Your lips
    have grit

sand
billowed down the
        beach
into my mouth

the rough grains
whipping across my calves,
       a lineage of sea cliffs
weathered
by this same easterly,
the homes of aquatic life
that took longer than
people have been writing love poems
to break down
into silt that later
           we will trail across my kitchen

in between your toes
is a testament to
       what was here before us
what will be,
afterwards

I feel the swell of your chest
under my hand
and when you tip my face up to yours
your forefingers so gently under my chin
I feel my axis tilt,
       the centre of myself
          shift

the water
        pushes and drags from the shore
but past the breaking waves
is a blue,
      flat calm.

To My Little Sister
(Who I Pretend Doesn't Exist)

You are auburn-haired and freckled like your mother;
she used to play an untuned piano,
I remember her pale, slender
fingers flying over the yellowing keys.

When she was pregnant with you,
she craved radishes sprinkled with salt,
and if I was present for photos,
she required two –
one I would join her family in,
and another I would watch
from out of shot.

The house you all lived in
had leadlight windows and an open fireplace,
a flinching red kelpie,
and a giant elm tree out back.

My memories of our father are sharp but intermittent,
a stitch jabbing under my ribs:
car rides alone with him,
the hot leather seat licking
the backs of my legs,
the half-centimetre gap between his front teeth,
his love of chocolate éclair ice-cream,
and his surprising and irrational
hatred of *Mr Bean*.

I still see his calloused
hands rolling up ciggies,
the way he carefully brought
the edge of the rice paper to his tongue,
feel the clotting in my stomach,

when he came in
to say goodnight.

Communion

the citric smell of wild thyme
rose in the dry heat of the day
its crisp little leaves
crunching with each step
as I climbed down a clay gully
to be lakeside
      with you
to let your skin
        speak to mine
let your flesh say
           nice things
           secrets
           praise
on a rug of pine needles

you held my face
handfuls of hair
         you are what I need
your body said
as it drove further into mine

the pile left our backs scratched
and sharp indentations
pressed into my knees

later, at home
I ate hunks of bread
and in the mirror
each red line across my skin
I said a prayer for

Te Anau

We climb through cold, dank tunnels
to pile into a small boat with eight strangers
I clutch at you
there is darkness and water
                              whirling below us

I can smell your treacle breath
as you tilt my chin to the roof of the cave
where constellations of worms
lit themselves from within

despite these beautiful
pinpricks in the blackness
I feel my mind reach for common things:
the dress I wanted but never bought
what we will eat for breakfast tomorrow
that I didn't buy milk
the time I picked the quick of my nails
right before a meeting
and had to negotiate
shaking strange hands with bloody fingertips

insignificant regrets
small pangs in the silence
even with worms
making a Milky Way above us
I carried the dullness of my being
through Southland
over the sound, past the beechwood trees
and into this hollow rock

the guide asked us
to leave no trace of ourselves here
but I drop those invisible aching details

to the limestone floor
as we make our way out
under insect starlight.

Cardiogenic Words

Your inner iris
    is a yellow halo
        your pupils dance in and out of
as you sit next to me
under harsh morning sun
on the waterfront of Lake Wakatipu.

You taste of Pimm's and cucumber,
and smell of salt and oranges.
Squinting at me with those golden green eyes,
you place your cool hand
        gently on my sunburnt neck.

You say, *'I love you'*.

I flutter.
    The red elasticity of my heart
        stretches and pulls
through each beat.
    Heat spreads
      over my skin like coffee,
            spilt.
I feel the muscle in my chest
pumping blood so fast,
its hot liquid in my veins,
a blue flame in my stomach.

Your words stoke me,
overturning embers
inside my chest.

Hypnic Jerk

I have kept
    dream souvenirs
for a time when remembering you
wouldn't grow an apple
    in my throat

standing behind me
your hands in the sink
washing dirty plates you couldn't see
    your lips a sweet bruise on my neck

your soapy soft hands
    and my milk pink nipples
the way they slipped
    so easily into your mouth

how cool the granite benchtop felt
under my palms
the moment of hesitation
that slight pause
when you asked if this was okay

unnoticed

we were missing
each other
    already

kitchen sex
was dream-falling
the same wild shudder
jerking me
awake.

Party After Riccarton Races

The courtyard is lined with tall, dark elms
and people who are all perfume and teeth,
holding conversations about
building houses and places to honeymoon,
lush-sounding places,
like Palenque and Lucca, that might end up
the names of
their first-born children.

There's a pool, and immediately
I want to slide my dress off my shoulders
and slip into the cool blue novelty, instead
I find myself wandering upstairs
alone, shoes off,
going into empty bedrooms and bathrooms,
surprised to recognise
soap and shampoo
from supermarket aisles.

I find a quivering dachshund in the laundry –
I call her Sarah,
that's what rich people call their dogs.
Sarah and I have words
about the bourgeoisie,
and when I emerge
white lines are being passed around on platters
like cheese and crackers,
perfectly ordered parallel stripes,
as if some poor sucker out the back
was charged with the job of
arranging the narcotics,
and I notice nothing gets smoked here,
just snorted, a classist etiquette
for substance abuse.

Sunday, without sleep,
I seek out the beach, hope
that sand on skin might release
the brine in my head.

Walking along the esplanade,
the easterly cutting through my clothes,
all I could think was
rich people use Palmolive too.

Knots

my body
lies twisted
a jumble of limbs and hair
inside my head

I slide two fingers
down my throat
to ease out the knots
I have folded myself into
starting gently
at the bottom
and working my way up
just like
when I sat on his knee
at six years old
and he carefully combed
my tangled blonde curls

his wide, hard hands
surprisingly gentle
but his knee
slowly grinding
underneath me.

Kitchen Sink

Purging
at the kitchen sink
until I am damp with sweat
empty
knuckle white grip on the lip
                    of the bench

in the window's condensation
a glass haze of who I guess I am now
ashen
        trembling

the food comes up
easily enough, cold water
goes down and my fingers go back,
it rushes up
again
again

then, perhaps
a small hope,
fragile and easily lost
like the silver butterflies that hold earrings in my ears
and when dropped
are only able to be found again when the light
catches them
just right,
that I might expel this wave of dread,
if my fingers could reach
        down
            far enough
this dark adrenalin might rush into my mouth
sticky, bitter tar

and be
gone.

My grandmother refers to her stomach
as her spare tire,
and her handbag
as the kitchen sink,
always rebuking herself for carrying
so much that is heavy, unnecessary

I lug my own kitchen sink with me

I hold his name in my mouth
until I feel the swell start in my stomach
lean forward,
again

Camping on Banks Peninsula

Wind hits the blonde seeding grass,
and the temperature drops
in increments of degrees,
every hair is a fine needle
standing at attention
in the follicles of my bare arms.

Light wisps through the leaves of the white
pine above us,
dappled.
The word fills my mouth like honey;
I breathe it: 'dappled'.

You say,
'what?'

Our tent is a hot plastic den
so we lie outside as night
pours into the sky.

You see the Southern Cross.

I see battlefields,
glaciers carving out rivers,
altars and spires, lions,
lines on the faces of mothers,
mountains shifting,
artists painting lovers,
living rooms and TV dinners.

I watch stars knit together
like bones mending
to tell tales
of deserts blossoming and oceans waning,

the permanence of
everything earthen
fading.

Our insignificance
is strung in the stars,
the shimmering expanse
a reassurance of my own fragility.

You point out Orion's sword,
and I feel your smile cut
through the dark.

Nearly

it was winter
the six weeks I carried you

I didn't know you were with me
yet I felt your absence acutely
a hollow pain burrowing
        from my back to my pelvis

we drove in slow silence
over black ice
while you unfurled
inside me

now, in a café by the water
our glasses filled with Prosecco
pink from raspberries
I tell my girlfriend how it was
to feel the presence of your brief life
only in traces of its absence
to untangle sadness and relief
from a knot
inside myself

we sip and sigh

this part I don't share:
under clear September skies
before bare trees
boast their soft adornment
morning air is cold shrapnel
a sharp twinge in my chest
for who we might have been

when green shoots emerge
despite frost and hard ground
missing you
hurts the same way
a broken
bone aches
before
the rain.

Loving a Depressive

He says my love is worth its weight
(it's just getting so heavy to carry).

I want him to hold my soul, grip-tight,
but his touch is light.
He grasps me by the edges
like I am delicate, soiled tissue
as if whatever darkness is inside me
might be catching.

I crave his embrace
but feel him bracing.
He thinks closeness is being the styrofoam
in the box my fragile bones rattle around in.
He wants to wrap cotton around my thoughts,
but I like them jagged,
so pointed that sometimes they draw blood.

I'm the sharp stone in his shoe,
the craggy reminder of all things uncomfortable.
I'm the pebble he wants to sand the past from.
He wants me smooth enough to skim across cold lakes
but I don't bounce across the surface,
I am not afraid of the water
and I cannot exist in this world
without it touching me.

I draw baths full
of feelings,
soak in bubbles,
let the human experience soften my skin
and occasionally, I stay in a little too long
until the water goes grey and cold,
but I never ask him to drain it.

There are times quietness sets in on me,
a frost I wait to turn to dew.
I have a heart full of flowers
coloured with life,
but sometimes the blossoms
are suspended in an icy silence,
petals shimmering white;
and in that crystalline coldness I still
write him love poems
he hasn't earned yet.

Girlfriendship

Three women, not far off thirty,
are drinking tea the table over,
discussing their teenage masturbation habits.
I hear about carrots,
how their teenage selves
made Sims characters pash
and then curiously touched their breasts,
at the shared lounge-room computer.

They are laughing,
retelling stories of girlfriendship:
a doll called 'baby hot chips',
the smell of hair heating on a curling tong,
the sanctity of fried chicken Tuesdays,
memories of Barbie's perfect
cylindrical breasts,
the joy of
buying a pair for yourself.

I know these women:
they fold each other's washing
                              and thoughts,
they make emotional origami
from what it means to be a daughter,
to find love, to have doubt,
they crease paper sculptures
out of the life quivering in their stomach,
to want more, but to accept less;
the things we all do
to receive love.

Girlfriends hold each other,
not carefully, not by the edges,
but closely, forcefully,

each friend
an oath
pressed into the centre
of the other.

Waiuta

Everything damp.

The trail scattered with fragments
of the past:
a decaying coal trolley,
rotting water mill,
lone standing chimneys,
their red bricks peeking from behind lush scrub.

I chain smoke,
pick my cuticles
and feel myself changing colour,
viridescent.

Nearly 600 people lived here once;
now, native bush has taken lease
of these empty cottages,
and small insects
are the only inhabitants
crawling over my skin,
conversing with one another
on a frequency my ears can't tune to.

Rubies emerge in perfect droplets from my skin.
I smear them and my hands are red
                              and rust-smelling.

We sit on the rocky bank of Blackwater River.

The sun beats down,
a pulse
on the hot skin of my shoulders.

I feel the skeleton jitter inside me
and I worry it might come loose.

I look to my sister,
waist-length red hair in a top knot,
her round green eyes
dilated different sizes.
One eye almost entirely pupil,
the other
a black pinprick surrounded by fern iris.

Her crooked gaze makes my tummy clench,
and an unstoppable something
roll up from my belly;
laughter.
Manic, wild,
eyes streaming and breath
evading.

We stick to sidelong glances
and share long slices of havarti cheese.

He gives me his favourite cardigan.
It's lined with satin and
the large metal buttons
cold and smooth on my fingertips.
He says it will make me calm;
so it does.

I think of the men who might've eaten here
when this was a bustling mining town,
hard-working men
with dense palms and paper lungs,
who went underground for aurum,
inhaling quartz dust
in exchange for potential prosperity.

I see them,
in flannel and moleskin,
grit caught in the lines on their faces,
pronouncing their frowns and smiles –
a crew of pantomime labourers
eating lunch on the Blackwater riverbank.

They are watching water dance
over these same brown stones,
leaving coal-stained fingerprints
on the bread of their sandwiches
and breathing fresh, cool air,
before returning to the
dark pit
of the mine.

Amitriptyline Dreams

when my left temple broke my fall
I spent months
            watching food grow cold
            sitting in my parked car in the dark
and weeks suspended in a search of objects
            I couldn't remember where I put them, and then
what it was I was looking for

the backs of my hands were smudged
            with lists:
buy bread, the doctor's name, chores to be done

I found myself
            walking through cemeteries at night
standing in my garden
            barefoot on the cold grass, in first light
laying on the bedroom floor
                        these things were a strange comfort

one specialist prescribed tiny blue pills
for the ache behind my eyes
                        'a-mi-TRIP-ti-leen'
and the dreams came
one after the other
an impatient queue of my own concealments

cutting in front was pulling my hair
            into a ponytail
only to discover my scalp descended
                        well below my shoulders

next Muscovy ducks pushed past
their fleshy red bills
            hissing at my heels

a baby was passed down the line
perfectly formed, but impossibly small
I cradled her in my palm
as she slowly
        turned blue

then, a gargantuan black dog
        chewing yellow freesias in my garden
and knowing he would gnaw on my bones
        I let him in

at the back of the crowd
eerily quiet, the dining table stood alone
covered in my fingernails and fillings
picked and arranged
        into one last poem

Concussion

you visit Tuesday after the accident,
arms full of pink stargazers
            and crossword puzzles

asking about my slip tentatively,
a tight-lipped smile
as you silently recount the story
I have told other friends

I speak deliberately,
whilst there is no trace of fracture in my voice,
no kiss of bruising on my temple,
I haven't yet returned home
                    to myself

wet clay, I say,
            and then the fall,
though I only felt the
                    landing

clay, you repeat slowly,
and I wonder if you're remembering
pottery classes at night school
where we learnt how
clay grips on to the life
                worked into it

        you can wedge and throw it,
yet somehow clay will recall
            how soft your touch was
                        in the beginning,
            its molecules still feeling
                    where your gentle hands faulted,
                        before the
                                    fire

Calling Hours

A strange day,
the kind you want to put an end to,
and I do, sitting on the kitchen floor,
drunk and eating a $12 jar
of maraschino cherries

bright saccharine orbs,
their decay suspended in sweetness,
remind me of the morning viewing
of my grandfather's preserved body,
his bluish lips bared in a waxen grimace

and there was my aunty,
more than twenty years passed
since she let me blow out her birthday candles,
those decades not so easy for her,
her arm hanging limply at her side

behind the casket was the dining-room cabinet,
home to porcelain figures that Granny bought
in mourning of her daughter's mobility,
movement and drape captured in their dresses,
mirror images of each other,
slim and long-limbed,
they stand protected behind glass,
symbolic of my aunt's departed elegance

she drags her foot behind her, stubborn-streaked
and gap-toothed like her father and brother,
you're not like them
Granny murmured to me as I said goodbye

what a funny thing it is
to share blood and not much else,

and that's not to say I don't like them,
just that I don't know them,
and yet in my grandparents' lounge
there they all were,
making coffee and space for me
in the most intimate corner
of their lives.

Lost Friend

you are my dream-teeth crumbling
the puddle of an unfinished poem
green juniper berries
his wilting mouth on my neck
a horse lying down
the rash creeping between my fingers
a pyre
my mother, holding me
my mother, turning away
the knot of cells coming undone in my belly
Braille painted with oleander sap
the hidden pink and fleshy patch of my scalp
wreaths of white flowers, bought to be buried
the smell of an ex-lover on a stranger's skin
a slap dressed as a hug
a pinch of spilt salt flying over my left shoulder
a match under the gas
an empty blue eggshell
a pile of orange stamen, pulled from fresh lilies
you are missing yet still here
you are a list, not a poem
a collection of things that do not correspond
a puzzle I cannot make sense of

and I love you, still.

Panic

Clenching my hands
my fingernails leave
purple crescents on my palms.

I count my ribs,
my dog's shallow breathing.

I want to open my forearm like a letter;
I imagine the skin unzipping neatly
to reveal men,
digging out words from my flesh with
picks and shovels.

My body is a colliery,
for memories I never put on the page,
thoughts that never made it to my mouth.

I rest my hand on my dog's warm side;
I look for comfort
in the wire of her fur.

The miners tunnel through
the depths of my tissue,
and into the shallow pit of my stomach.

Their spoils are my poems:
coal embers, lit from within,
verses that glow in their beginnings,
and fade as they lose their way.

My breath cuts short
and acidic run-off fills my mouth.

I feel the world's smallest
canary die inside me.

His yellow body
growing stiff and cold,
a tiny feathered knot
in the left atrium
of my heart.

Mickel

When I dream of you now, there's a child on your hip,
your milk has come in, your husband tells you it is sweet
as he gently puts the pink bud
of your nipple in his mouth.

You're a mother, a lover,
running a household and an office,
drinking wine (but only riesling), your dark brown hair
shining at your shoulders.

You still laugh the same, Mickel,
but your eyes crinkle at the corners.
In my sleep, I see you beautiful in a different way,
your body lived-in, your life brimming
with everything we wanted for each other,
when we were just girls,
crowded around your hospital bed,
feeling the cold touch of grief
for the first time.

Guilt Trip

Kaikōura, pre-quake,
        winding up green hills,
we hold hands and
             fragile moments.

Playing pretend with a weekend escape
in a sad little studio apartment,
        water stains and a mauve bedspread,
                Bible on the side table.
I take a photo,
        in the reflection of my sunglasses,
              his hand on my leg.

        I am wavering.

We climb to Ōhau Point
in search of seal pups,
        find the waterfall empty.

We walk the rocky coastline,
watching tourists watching seals.
A French woman asks us about 'penguineses'.
        We laugh.
        We lose it,
        like we are on drugs,
             like it's much funnier than it actually is.

I see the seals as they are:
swaddled in thick layers of blubber,
rolls of fat where a neck would be,
        lazy,
             yet fiercely volatile.

Their smell hangs in the air:
salt, ammonia, rotting fish.

Cry, Babe

My best friend cries because
rabbits can't get married,
she cries because of volunteer potatoes,
for the yellow of mustard flowers,
and she tears up when she tells me
that children's dictionaries
no longer contain the word catkin,
catkins, she says,
   hang from the sweet chestnut tree in her garden
self-contained stems of down
that need nothing but the wind to make love to themselves,
she is so sad that children won't know
the name of these non-gender-binary,
     self-perpetuating flowers.

She drinks three quarters of her glass of merlot,
tells me she is going to write a poem
     about the godwits.
I say I'm going to write a poem
about her writing a poem
     about the godwits;
     she tells me that's been done.

When we were seven
she had a popsicle-stick graveyard
for dead houseplants,
her mother said a few words
at the internment of a maiden fern,
who met its shrivelled end
in the corner of the guest room.

Each wooden cross had a
name scrawled in biro,
and with salted cheeks,

61

wearing the only black we had,
we clasped our small hands
together in solemn prayer
for the forgotten houseplants,
the faceless, indoor greenery
        that she loved
                with her entire
                little being.

Saturday Night
in the Emergency Department

Tannins cling to my teeth
from washing down sedatives
with too much tempranillo,
my molars are bitter stones in the back of my mouth
and my sister cradles the crook of my arm.
Her palms are small and damp,
how they have been since we were six.

There's a young man,
hand wrapped in a blood-soaked T-shirt,
explaining to the registrar
the stakes of tonight's beer-pong tournament,
that if he lost, he would've had to drink
fluid from an old bong,
as he illustrates the physical nature of the game,
his blood lands in scarlet tears on the dirty linoleum
and quietly next to us
an Indian girl wearing pink and white striped leggings
fingers the gold chain around her father's neck;
he smells like sandalwood and worry.

Hanging on one of the yellowing walls
is an oversaturated photo of hay bales,
printed and stretched over canvas,
the straw glows under a cerulean sky
and I can't say if it's with radiance or radiation,
or if the hospital interior designer
had hoped this psychedelic farm scene
might transpose waiting patients
from their beige plastic chairs, the lumps in their throats
and this hospital smell –
disinfectant, latex
and sick people,

circulated and recirculated –
to a world of agriculture in hyper-brilliance,
or if, perhaps, this was just the cheapest wall hanging she
could find,
after all, they don't mount Rousseau
in public hospitals.

We swing through the double doors
when they finally mispronounce my name.
The nurse is called Keith, sixty-something,
5'3" with a white buzz cut
and a silver stud winking in his ear.
He is on the twelfth tired hour of his shift,
but is gentle when he draws blood
from my scratched up arms,
and asks again,
why did you do this?
and what can I say.

Inside my body, something shook
so violently I wanted to split it from myself.
The silver edge of the knife ran down my wrist
with all the cool relief of tap water on a too-hot day,
and in one moment,
with a man I hardly knew,
horror licked my brain like a blue flame,
and I didn't care anymore,
to breathe, or to laugh so much I snort,
or greet my dog after a long day,
that I couldn't face another drive to the office, another meal,
another conversation of 'I'm well thanks, what about you?'
another series of moments when I wonder
why sometimes,
just *being*
hurts like a
stomach full
of sand.

Duck Hunting

Our final visit to Rakaia huts
was in duck-hunting season

we lay in bed, the thin red
curtains casting us burgundy
as shots jarred the static morning
air, and dogs barked in the distance

conversation was laborious
at the lagoon, thermos in hand and dragging
your toes through the dust
you winced when the young man
on the water used his whistle
to lure the fat birds
                    into flight

it was a week after my birthday
the night you didn't come home
when I rang the hospital
panicked you may have been in an accident
later, you would admit
it was the first time you fucked her
out the back of the party, on the grass

I had washed the dirt
                    from your jeans

that afternoon I walked
on the beach alone
saw the feathered bodies
of two mallards,
            metres apart
their ordinary mottle brown
clipped by lead

what startled me
was the deep purple of their specula
against the greywacke beach
somehow iridescent and
                                    lifeless

Descent into Poetry

on dark days
poems come
damp, smelling of bile
salt-skinned, ruddy-cheeked
a perfect scarlet line streaking down my leg
they come flawed
dimples, stretch marks
and too many adjectives

badly written sonnets
emerge from piles of unwashed clothes
I find haikus
growing on cheese in the back of the fridge
derivative metaphors
appear on the misted bathroom mirror
and words run out of the shower
washing over me as I grow cold
words like
gossamer, halcyon, filament
but also
gut, bleach, rancid,
the temperature of the water slowly
                              dropping
as it falls
down my back

I contemplate
getting dressed
while I count syllables
and search for synonyms
for words like
despair.

The Night I Knew I Had to Leave My Man

in the bathroom,
like so many times before

I still feel the cold linoleum
below the pads of my feet,
the geography of his chest
under my palms,
the tightness of my scalp
as his hand
grabbed a fistful of my hair
and bowed me forward

I was so malleable then,
a hot spoon
forced through hard ice-cream,
buckling

against the glass
my forehead pressed on its sharp edge
like brain freeze,
one thought held in my mind
like the breath in my lungs
it will be over
    soon

my fear was dry and sour-tasting,
my tongue
foreign to the rest of my mouth,
and in the reflection
of the mirrored cabinet
I watched his eyes on me,
dark, narrow,
unseeing

his metal bending
was usually by psychokinesis

he disguised friends as traitors
shuffled my words like a cold deck
he lay silence over me for weeks
only to yank the blanket back
just before I vanished
                              completely

a glare, a pause
clearing his throat
could saw me in half
                              quarters
                              eighths

it was the distortion of matter
without physical pressure
like a magician from the seventies
proving his power by
twisting silverware
with his mind

I still feel myself, raw
as I sat on the lip of the bath,
the ceramic cool underneath me

I remember the smell of us,
and my hand feeling
for blood

I often think of my quiet passivity,
the quiver of my hands
and my voice,
when it was over
asking
            why?

his reply,
that he was
trying
to love
me

I dream of drawers
full of warped spoons;
once bent,
always a little
misshapen.

Morning After

I wake to synthetic apples
                    and the musk of the mildew
creeping up these peeling walls

You're vaping
                    sun seeping through the leadlight glass
                              washing you flat blue

The house shifts and sighs
                              gently

There's a chandelier:
          a monument to changing taste
          a home for spiders
          a place for dust to collect itself

Before I go
          I drink you in
                    the last time

I hold you
          and this moment in my mouth,
swill around all we have left,
stale sheets, the dampness of the mattress
seeping through to my back,
your soft hair tousled,
candy breath making the window blush,
your moon-shaped face,
                    tinted blue.

The Last Part of Leaving

I had to go back for the remainders
piling books, pots and pans
dresses into the car
things I hadn't needed for months
but didn't want to abandon

it was hurried
as if he was there
hanging in the curtains
his shadow on the driveway
reductive hints of him
in the empty green bottles
dishes covered in dried food,
clothes strewn
carelessly across the floor

he was growing in the lush
thicket that seized the garden
in the blight creeping up the windows
and as I was packing the last carload
his smell snuck up on me
in the hallway, diesel cologne
the one in a glass clenched fist
malted barley, marijuana

unfinished arguments tugged at my
sleeve
the disarray pleaded at my feet
and I stood in the doorway
making silent bargains
with broken furniture

in the end I went back inside
prayed on my knees

burnt sage in each room
let the wind in, and
when I finally locked up
placed the key under the mat
I heard the house gasp
stay.

I enjoy listening to sad songs

The Following Summer

That December was heavy, thick
I felt myself weighted,
struggling to move through air
I was underwater with open eyes
breathless and pressurised
seeing everything through
the blur and sting
                    of seawater

My new breasts were tight and hard in my chest
and I had to sleep on my back for the first time
my body an unfamiliar collection of bones,
brittle as shells, and freshly bleached hair.

It was an achingly empty summer
it was bitten, itchy skin
damp thighs rubbing on denim
it was bare chested and freckled
salt licking new scars

It was the season of lemons
softening in the bowl
damp fur, and fingernails bitter and green
from tearing and linking
                    daisy stems

it was clotted blood, sprinklers
strawberries and razor blades
it was warm, long nights alone

It was the summer of the 6 a.m. hate poem
the first season the soles of my feet
                    grew thick and hard
and as I watched shadows stretch

and felt cool wind come off the water
it was the summer
I fell in love with
                myself.

Oracles and Crunchy Peanuts

Hannah has kind, coal eyes,
tells me my head is candyfloss pink:
you are fun,
but
someone has taught you
that you are not.

I knew the constellations.
Star maps on his back,
dulcet tones,
how to be light enough
to walk
carpets of eggshells.

She says my
tropical holiday
is what I need,
silicone and morphine,
everything yet to be seen.

On the plane ride,
the German couple next to me
couldn't believe
how the peanuts
were so fresh.

Moving In

I fill the house with books and cups of tea growing cold,
I sit in a stream of sunlight on the lounge floor,
I string up fairy lights,
and deadlock the door.

I tape poems on the cupboards,
the garden here is in bloom,
I cut fresh flowers,
rose and sweet pea follow me room to room.

I eat odd foods at odd times,
I can't sleep at night,
I play Joni Mitchell
and check the bulb in the floodlight.

I flatten boxes, find homes for picture hooks,
navigate new neighbours and streets,
cry on the phone to my internet provider,
make my old bed up with new sheets.

I hear the house and furniture lean in,
repeat my new mantra; *this is my fresh start*,
I have dreams of beginnings and endings,
          watching in slow motion, how it all fell apart.

For Chagall's Wife, Bella

I bring you bowls of lavender,
pale peace lilies, luminous trumpets,
long-stemmed red roses,
and white carnations.

For fourteen years I thought this painting
would remain unfinished,
but now, like you,
I put it to rest.

Dear wife, my flying lover,
in dreams I see you
          round and pale,
your cheeks and curls full,
your face shrouded by soft lace veil.

When we were young
the smell of rose hung heavier
than our bodies
in blue night air.

Your love was not a rooster
as big as the moon,
announcing itself every dawn.

It was tender, unassuming;
you held my soul
through each dark night
the way water
cups pale
moonlight.

Seeing My Father Across the Road
at Twenty-Seven

You've gotten soft, old man.
Your hair is silver wire.
Eighteen years on and
you got rid of the green car,
and your wife got rid of you.

I look different too:
the gap between my front teeth closed,
I got blonder, thinner,
I have fine lines around my eyes now
(I met a man just like you).

I have a proper job, a house, and a dog,
and I've not thought about you
                          too much Dad;
you can't miss what you never had.

You used to assemble boats on a factory line,
wear your hair long.
You practise tae kwon do like other men play golf,
and here you are,
smoking durries on your porch,
right over the road.

Your palms used to be
yellow from nicotine.
I bet they are the
hardest part of you, now.

Wild Poppies

Tonight,
I drink beer and
		walk my dog along
the red-zone riverside

I pluck beautiful weeds
	from the overgrown bank,
feel their vibrant crimson
		petals wilt in my hands

milk from poppy stems stain
		my palms yellow,
			edge my hands with a sharp bitterness

I watch the glass
		of the river
	break
		with drops of rain
before I feel its wet breath
on my skin.

Parting

My best friend's brother
walks me home
under low-hanging
orange sky;
a tangerine canopy
my fingertips can nearly
touch

the Canterbury nor'wester
wraps itself around my bare shoulders
and is perfumed with jasmine
and tobacco smoke

I note the crisp blue collar of Henry's shirt
matches his irises

the tar seal beneath my feet
is warm and soft from the sun,
we try to walk in unison,
a game in matching pace,
an attempt to synchronise ourselves,
like our identical steps
could be literal,
going forward
together

but he has a job at Oxford
and a girlfriend,
a fellow research fellow
with dark hair and
a name I would like to forget.

his strides are far longer
than mine anyway,

and though I enjoy pretending with each step,
I know it is pretend,
and we do not acknowledge
that one foot in front of the other
brings us closer
to goodbye

in the driveway,
shoes and wistful smiles in hand,
he leans me against the warm
summer-hill stone of my flat,
and pinning my wrists
to the rough brick and mortar,
presses his sandpaper chin
to mine

his tongue is hot syrup in my mouth and
sorrow is
powdered sugar
on my lips.

Searching for Gentleness

I spend Sunday
  searching the pink velvet of roses,
looking in the milky coffee cup rings
   I wipe from the kitchen table,
hopeful some might be tucked
into my purse, like a receipt,
  kept carefully, a thought to the future,
    to the brittleness of things.

I find a little
  in the warm wind
   that shakes petals from the wild plum trees
    along the cycleway,
and I feel some,
  in the wet stamp
   of my dog's nose.

I close my eyes and the cyclists ride on past.

Craving,
  I pull out clothes from my wardrobe,
discard the things that do not bring me joy,
  a heap of defeated pastels on my bedroom floor.

I check the spaces you left,
  the small gaps in my life that are mending,
filled with time and the shapes of other men,
  I linger on the front steps where we smoked Dunhill blues,
felt the heat of our bodies leech into the concrete.

I trawl the sunlight
  that streams into my lounge at 7 p.m.,
   the lukewarm tea I brew for myself,

and slowly the rough edges
of today
soften.

Dead Man's Point

Autumnal Central Otago
copper poplars line Lake Dunstan,
a pool of glass underneath
this Southern watercolour sky

the yolk yellow leaves,
brash and unashamedly golden
in this lilac light,
are shocking in their defiance
of the gentle pastel landscape

they stir something inside me
that has lain still
                              for so long.

Slaughter
in response to 'Pig Hunting' by Rachel Bush

you were hunting for a poem
and found a pig
swaddled in thick layers of chub
her brown eyes,
dark pools, pale lashes;
soft, immense, beautiful

but there is no note
of her thoughtfulness,
the grunts in different tones
      'pleased to see you'
      'no more cabbage thanks'
      'I am terribly sorry for eating the peonies'

nor did you include *why* she is in your stable,
you did not tell us about
the silver blade under her hairy jowls
her shrill scream
the Mexican blanket,
logs from the peach tree,
sprayed with crimson

that you will eat your poem

there was no mention of
the metallic tang
that will hang
in the air.

What I Would Say to Him, Now

I have to look through photographs
to remember the angles of your face,
the line of your jaw, exact hazel of your eyes.

I can only picture outlines,
the edges of you,
around which I was allowed to exist.

You're a Monet,
a blurred impressionism,
a swirl of colour and a tummy ache.

At night while I wait for my tablets to work,
inkblots float behind my eyelids.
Shapes and colours of you
whirr around the darkness of my skull.

Our familiarity,
foreign.

My meds should ease me into sleep
and blunt the sharp pangs of my sadness,
but sometimes I can't endure
how it sanitises my emotions,
making them like my memories of you.

I take steps towards self-care.

I walk our little terrier,
and in the pale winter sky
suspended above us
black branches of deciduous trees
spread like veins of ink through the twilight.

I think my anxiety is dark wood
growing and grafting through my mind,
tangling itself in any remaining clarity.

It's getting late.

What I really want to ask is: do you remember
the rush of our bodies, palms and hips beating,
when you kissed me the first time?

Can you recall the bitingly cold June nights we spent,
six years ago, in the back of your father's truck,
our breath hanging in the air,
like unsaid words between us?

The morning is clear and cold. I feel alive, again.

I still find shards of who I was to you, buried in my body,
I can't bear to dig them out completely.

Can you tell me if you were certain,
when you slipped the ring on my finger,
one knee in the tawny sand?

How sweet your fingers were
when you pulled apart peonies and
scattered the apricot petals on our sheets.

How did I go from everything
to nothing at all?

Mary, from Timaru

Developed by the good folks
in Devon Street, New Plymouth
masters of miniature camera
there she is, swimming
in that plush fur coat,
wide lipstick smile with
too many teeth (like mine).

Standing outside a hall,
there for a dance, her carefully
pencilled brows raised
to whoever is left of the cameraman.

Hanging from her ears
are large plastic suns. She clutches
a small glass of mother's ruin
and a durry in one hand,
her other hand
grips her own wrist,
tight.

Mary, sometimes Shayna,
the woman who needed two names,
the reason my father hates women
with such violence,
my grandmother.

I met her once.
She gave me melon-scented soaps,
her curls were fire-truck red,
she smelt like smokes
and cooking fat.

Twenty-Seventh Christmas

I woke up alone in my new house
at 5
took a valium
woke again at 10

poured amaretto into my cup of tea
sat on the floor in my bedroom
felt the neon vacancy signs inside me light up
advertising positions left unfilled
partner, mother, father, siblings
lit up,
got lit

took deep breaths
didn't wash my hair
applied bright pink lipstick
practised smiling
put in my silver ladybird earrings
changed my top
gave my dog two presents
watched her play with them
ached a little more

thought about peace on earth
and in closed garages
with engines left running,
warm baths blossoming like blushing faces
long sleeps

put on shoes
ate cheese
watched my dog eat cheese
drank a beer

wrote a list
pretended the list was a poem

wished I had something
more profound to say
than this.

Palmistry

My grandmother has tissue-paper hands.
The backs of them soft, blackened,
like overripe fruit,
on her ring finger,
three solitaire diamonds
worn decades longer as a widow
than a wife.

These hands used to fly over piano keys,
fry segg fritters — the smell
of hot butter permeating the house —
plait my damp flaxen hair into tiny braids,
carefully tying the ends of them in pink wool,
unravelling them in the morning.

Her gnarled knuckles raised three children,
two her own, and then
my mother, a redhead
with a stutter and a sweet tooth,
who always felt out of place.

They moved over the body of her husband
intimately, obligingly,
despite his adulteries,
and then gently, changing
his colostomy bag.

Before carpal tunnel and arthritis invaded,
these hands expertly pruned roses,
her favourite, a fuchsia
called *Maggie Barry*,
and they would slice red strawberries
from her garden into bowls
of vanilla ice-cream; we would slurp up

sweetness
on her sunny patio.

When we say grace,
she declares that I have cold hands, and
a warm heart; *don't go giving it all away.*

My grandmother has perfect fingernails,
her lined palms are soft, fleshy,
as they rest tenderly
on my arm; her touch
feels like home.

My Honest Poem
based on Rudy Francisco's 'My Honest Poem'

I was a winter baby. Born on July fourth.
My birth stone is the ruby.
I'm 5'3". I don't sleep much.

I have no sense of direction.
I get lost in lovers
like they are unfamiliar cities. I rush in
like a middle-aged woman
at the Ballantynes sale.

My favourite smell is fresh
mandarin rind, and clean washing
straight off the line, sunshine
still lingering in the fibres.

The sound I like best is the morning
at 6 a.m., which doesn't sound like
much at all.

My umbilical cord was tied
around my neck when I was born;
I've been blue and breathless ever since.
These aren't my real lips.

I like cups of tea almost as much as
I like lorazepam.

I prefer 'exquisitely sensitive' to anxious. I've got markers
for the rise and quell of my sanity; from peeling
poems off my fingers to watching spiders,
fat as babes, crawl across my ceiling.

Sometimes I wonder what my dog says about me
when I'm not around. I suspect she jokes
that I don't get driven mad anymore; lunacy
is in walking distance.

Hi, my name is Jess. Jessica's
too roomy.

I enjoy ice-cream on cold days, listening to sad songs
and sitting cross-legged on the floor
of bookshops.

My hobbies include reading other people's horoscopes,
putting flowers in road cones and trying to
talk myself down from the steep cliffs
of my own panic.

When I was a scrap of blonde hair, pink cheeks
and jam-smeared hands, my grandma would say
'that girl always needs a pen in her hand'
and at twenty-eight, I think she called it,
right from the start.